BOUNDARIES IN MARRIAGE

PARTICIPANT'S GUIDE

Resources by Henry Cloud and John Townsend

Books

Boundaries (and workbook)
Boundaries in Dating (and workbook)
Boundaries in Marriage (and workbook)
Boundaries with Kids (and workbook)
Boundaries with Teens (Townsend)
Changes That Heal (and workbook) (Cloud)
Hiding from Love (Townsend)
How People Grow (and workbook)
How to Have That Difficult Conversation You've Been Avoiding
Making Small Groups Work
The Mom Factor (and workbook)
Raising Great Kids
Raising Great Kids Workbook for Parents of Preschoolers
Raising Great Kids Workbook for Parents of School-Age Children
Raising Great Kids Workbook for Parents of Teenagers
Safe People (and workbook)
12 "Christian" Beliefs That Can Drive You Crazy

Video Curriculum

Boundaries
Boundaries in Dating
Boundaries in Marriage
Boundaries with Kids
Raising Great Kids for Parents of Preschoolers
ReGroup (with Bill Donahue)

Audio

Boundaries
Boundaries in Dating
Boundaries in Marriage
Boundaries with Kids
Boundaries with Teens (Townsend)
Changes That Heal (Cloud)
How People Grow
How to Have That Difficult Conversation You've Been Avoiding
Making Small Groups Work
The Mom Factor
Raising Great Kids

BOUNDARIES IN MARRIAGE

PARTICIPANT'S GUIDE

AN 8-SESSION FOCUS ON
UNDERSTANDING
THE CHOICES
THAT MAKE OR BREAK
LOVING RELATIONSHIPS

DR. HENRY CLOUD & DR. JOHN TOWNSEND

WITH LISA GUEST

ZONDERVAN®

ZONDERVAN.com/
AUTHORTRACKER
follow your favorite authors

We want to hear from you. Please send your comments about this book to us in care of zreview@zondervan.com. Thank you.

ZONDERVAN®

Boundaries in Marriage Participant's Guide
Copyright © 2002 by Henry Cloud and John Townsend

Requests for information should be addressed to:

Zondervan, *Grand Rapids, Michigan 49530*

ISBN 978-0-310-24615-2

All Scripture quotations, unless otherwise indicated, are taken from the *Holy Bible, New International Version®*. NIV®. Copyright © 1973, 1978, 1984 by International Bible Society. Used by permission of Zondervan. All rights reserved.

Internet addresses (websites, blogs, etc.) and telephone numbers printed in this book are offered as a resource to you. These are not intended in any way to be or imply an endorsement on the part of Zondervan, nor do we vouch for the content of these sites and numbers for the life of this book.

Published in association with Yates & Yates, www.yates2.com.

Printed in the United States of America

HB 11.10.2023

Contents

Love Is Not Enough

*I*f you are reading this book, most likely marriage is important to you. You may be happy in your marriage and want to keep it growing. You may be struggling, dealing with major or minor problems. You may be single and want to prepare for marriage. You may even be divorced and want to prevent the pain you went through if you decide to remarry.

A lifetime of love and commitment to one person is one of the greatest gifts God has given us. Marriage is one of God's best designs; it's the one he chose as the metaphor to describe our relationship with him. It is the mystery of living as one flesh with another human being (Ephesians 5:31–32).

Marriage is about love. It is about being bound together by the care, need, companionship, and values of two people, which can overcome hurt, immaturity, and selfishness to form something better than what each person alone can produce. Love is at the heart of marriage, as it is at the heart of God himself (1 John 4:16).

Although love is at the heart of marriage, it is not enough. The marriage relationship needs other ingredients to grow and thrive. These ingredients are freedom and responsibility. When two people are free to disagree, they are free to love. When they are not free, they live in fear, and love dies. When two people together take responsibility to do what is best for the marriage, love can grow. When they do not, one takes on too much responsibility and resents it; the other does not take on enough and becomes self-centered or controlling.

This video curriculum is about promoting, growing, developing, and repairing love in a marriage. We want to help you strengthen your love for your spouse by providing a better environment for it: one of freedom and responsibility. This is where boundaries, or personal property lines, come in. They promote love by protecting individuals.

We need to make clear that this *Boundaries in Marriage* curriculum is not about fixing, changing, or punishing your mate. If you aren't in control of yourself, the solution is not learning to control someone else. The solution is learning self-control.

Instead, this curriculum is about taking ownership of your own life so that you are protected and you can love and protect your spouse without enabling or rescuing him or her.

Finally, today is the day to work on your own boundaries in marriage. What you take the initiative to deal with today will affect the rest of your married life. And what you ignore or are afraid to address will do the same.

So, welcome to the *Boundaries in Marriage* curriculum! We hope this is a helpful resource for you, whatever condition your marriage is in. We pray that as you learn to make the word *boundaries* a good word in your marriage, responsibility and freedom will then help love take root in both of your hearts. God bless you.

Henry Cloud, PhD
John Townsend, PhD

What's a Boundary, Anyway?

OVERVIEW

In this session, you will

- See that love, freedom, and responsibility are necessary ingredients if a marriage is to grow and thrive.

- Define "boundaries," look at examples of boundaries, and consider their importance.

- Recognize that you are responsible for your feelings, attitudes, beliefs, behaviors, choices, thoughts, values, limits, talents, desires, and love, all of which lie within your boundaries.

VIDEO SEGMENT

Stephanie's Story

- Freedom, responsibility, and love—something incredible happens as these three ingredients of relationship work together.

- Stephanie was suffering from the emotional distance that being on the wrong side of a one-sided relationship creates.

- Stephanie realized that there was really very little of her in the marriage. She had adapted to her husband and had complied with him so much that she could no longer even remember what it felt like to be herself.

- Stephanie realized that she could not blame Steve for her loss of herself. She was the one who, afraid of conflict, had complied with his wishes. She had to take ownership of her passivity.

- Stephanie took responsibility for her own misery and began to work on it in the relationship. She didn't—as many people do—leave the relationship to "find herself."

- As Stephanie took ownership and responsibility for her life, Steve was forced to take responsibility for his own, and their marriage improved.

- Steve also learned to love Stephanie's freedom. He began to be attracted by her independence instead of threatened by it.

TIME FOR THOUGHT
A Look in the Mirror

DIRECTIONS

You will be doing this exercise on your own. Take 5 minutes to answer the questions below and reflect on your own marriage.

1. What, if anything, did you see of yourself and your marriage in Stephanie's situation?

2. If you were Stephanie, what could you do to improve your marriage?

3. If you were Steve, what would you want Stephanie to do to let you know that she is drifting away from you?

4. Why are you taking this *Boundaries in Marriage* course? What do you hope to learn?

VIDEO SEGMENT

Love, Freedom, and Responsibility

- Marriage is about love. But while love is indeed at the heart of marriage, it is not enough.

- The marriage relationship needs freedom and responsibility to grow and thrive.

- When two people are free to disagree, they are free to love. When they are not free, they live in fear, and love dies.

- When two people together take responsibility to do what is best for the marriage, love can grow. When they do not, one takes on too much responsibility and resents it; the other does not take on enough and becomes self-centered or controlling.

- This course is about promoting love, growing it, developing it, and repairing it. We want to help you develop love through providing a better environment for it: one of freedom and responsibility. This is where boundaries, or personal property lines, come in. They promote love by protecting individuals.

TIME TO TALK
Love, Freedom, and Responsibility

DIRECTIONS

With your spouse, turn to another couple near you and take 10 minutes to share your answers to the three questions listed below.

1. Marriage is about being bound together by the care, need, companionship, and values of two people, which can overcome hurt, immaturity, and selfishness to form something better than what each person alone can produce. Love is at the heart of marriage, as it is at the heart of God himself (1 John 4:16). When have you seen or perhaps even experienced the partnership of marriage being "something better than what each person alone can produce"? Give a specific example.

2. When two people are free to disagree, they are free to love. When they are not free, they live in fear, and love dies.

    • Why does genuine love allow the freedom to disagree?

    • What fears come into play when people are not free to disagree—and why do those fears cause love to die?

3. When two people together take responsibility to do what is best for their marriage, love can grow. When they do not, one takes on too much responsibility and resents it; the other does not take on enough and becomes self-centered or controlling. What, if anything, do you see about yourself, your marriage, and/or marriage in general when you look through the lens this statement offers?

VIDEO SEGMENT

Boundaries in Marriage

- For intimacy in marriage to develop and grow, there must be boundaries. A boundary is a property line. It denotes the beginning and the end of something.

- If I know where the boundaries are in our relationship, I know who "owns" things such as feelings, attitudes, and behaviors. I know to whom they "belong." And if there is a problem with one of those, I know to whom the problem belongs as well.

- A relationship like marriage requires each partner to have a sense of ownership of himself or herself. The first way in which clarifying boundaries helps us is to define where one person ends and the other begins. What is the problem, and where is it? Is it in you, or is it in me? If we can see that the problem is our problem and that we are responsible for it, then we are in the driver's seat of change.

- Three realities have existed since the beginning of time: freedom, responsibility, and love. God created us free. He gave us responsibility for our freedom. As responsible free agents, we are told to love him and each other.

- When spouses are free to not react to each other, each takes responsibility for his or her own issues and loves the other person even when he or she does not deserve it. Free from each other's control, each gives love to the other freely, and that love transforms the individuals and produces growth in their marriage.

- As Stephanie and Steve became more defined, they became two people who could love and be loved. They began to know and enjoy one another.

TIME TO ACT

Identifying My Property Lines

DIRECTIONS

Take 15 minutes to start reading through the questions below. They are designed to help you consider different types of boundaries, to see where your boundaries are, and to decide where you could shore them up. You won't have time to finish this exercise right now, but you'll be encouraged to do so in the Boundary Building section at the end of this session.

1. The most basic boundary is language. Your words help define you. They tell the other person who you are, what you believe, what you want, and what you don't.

    •   Give an example of boundary-setting words that you and your mate use occasionally, if not regularly.

    •   How do you respond when your spouse uses boundary-setting words?

    •   How does your spouse respond to your boundary-setting words?

    •   When have you chosen silence rather than boundary-setting words—and why? Be specific.

2. God's truth and principles provide the boundaries of our exis-
   tence, and as we live within this truth, we are safe. In addition,
   being honest and truthful about ourselves and what is going
   on in a relationship provides boundaries.

   • Which of God's principles are functioning well in your
     marriage? ("Do not lie," "Do not commit adultery," "Do
     not covet," "Give to others," "Love one another," "Be
     compassionate," and "Forgive" are some.) Which, if any,
     have been violated? What have been the consequences
     of that violation—and what might be done to get those
     boundaries back in place?

   • When, if ever, have you been aware of giving your mate a
     false impression of your feelings or your perspective on
     the relationship? Why did you choose to do so? What have
     been the consequences of your choice?

3. Consequences define what you will and will not allow yourself
   to be exposed to. When words fail to communicate, actions can.

   • When have the consequences of pain or loss helped you or
     your spouse better understand the other's boundaries?

   • In what current situation, if any, might the use of conse-
     quences be an effective communicator of your bound-
     aries? What would those consequences be?

4. A pure heart and the commitment to work on things are necessary as one follows the advice of Proverbs to "guard your heart" (4:23) with some emotional distance.

   - What risks come with a couple's establishment of emotional distance? And what possible benefits?

   - When, if ever, has emotional distance been a conscious and talked-about choice in your marriage? In what ways was your relationship stronger afterwards?

5. Sometimes, when all else fails, people must get away from each other until the hurt can stop. Distance can provide time to protect, time to think, time to heal, and time to learn new things.

   - When have you or someone you know needed to resort to physical distance to provide space for healing and/or safety to preserve partners and the marriage itself? Remember that physical distance can range from simply removing oneself from an argument to moving into a shelter with your children.

   - What risks come with a couple's establishment of physical distance? What possible benefits?

6. God has always provided help from his family to those who need it.

- Identify both some risks and some benefits of turning to other people.

- Who, if anyone, has helped you strengthen your boundaries? Whose care, support, teaching, and modeling might help you set and maintain healthy boundaries in your marriage? Where could you go to find such people?

7. Time to work out a conflict or to limit the conflict is another boundary that structures difficulties in relationships.
   - When, if ever, have you used time as a boundary in your marriage?

   - What current issue in your marriage could benefit from one of the following arrangements: giving yourself an allotted time to talk about certain things; setting a specific time to work on a particular issue instead of discussing it in the heat of the moment; establishing seasons for certain goals? Be specific about the issue and about the timing that might help you and your spouse deal with it.

Closing Prayer

Lord God, after just one session, I'm seeing more clearly what a high calling marriage is. In order for me to respond to that calling, please help me learn to take ownership of my feelings, attitudes, and behaviors; to take responsibility for my choices, desires, thoughts, values, talents, and love; and both to grant my spouse freedom and responsibly act on the freedom my spouse grants me. Please give me wisdom as I use words, truth, consequences, emotional distance, physical distance, other people, and time to build or strengthen boundaries.

I'm a bit nervous as I set out on this journey toward a healthier marriage, and I'm feeling more than a little vulnerable. I know that you'll be with me each step of the way, and may your presence give me hope and the willingness to proceed. As I submit myself to your transforming touch, I ask you to be at work in my mate even as you work to make me more like Christ—in whose name I pray. Amen.

Boundary Building

1. Boundaries in marriage is not about fixing, changing, or punishing your mate. If you aren't in control of yourself, the solution is not learning to control someone else; the solution is learning self-control.

   • What would you like to fix or change in your spouse or punish him/her for? Let go of those unhealthy and unhelpful goals by making them a topic of prayer. Confess these desires and ask God to be at work in your mate even as he works to transform you.

- What aspects of your role as husband or wife current-ly call for you to exercise greater self-control? Submit those to the Lord and his sanctifying, transforming touch.

2. Each spouse must take responsibility for the following things:

> Feelings
> Desires
> Attitudes
> Thoughts
> Behaviors
> Values
> Choices
> Talents
> Limits
> Love

- Look closely at the above list. In what areas are you not taking responsibility? (Could a close friend help you answer this question? Would your spouse be able to answer it if you risked asking an opinion?)

- What would responsibility in those areas look like?

- How might taking responsibility impact and improve your marriage?

3. Finish the Identifying My Property Lines exercise—and then act on some of the insights you have gained as you answered the questions.

Applying the Ten Laws of Boundaries to Marriage

OVERVIEW

In this session, you will

- Learn about the ten laws of boundaries in marriage.

- Begin to see how applying these laws will help you shape your marriage into one based on God's principles of relationship.

- Start considering what each law means specifically for you in your marriage as well as what challenges to growth each presents for you.

VIDEO SEGMENT

Five Laws of Boundaries

- Boundary issues in marriage always require an understanding of the specific marriage situation. In the long run, learning principles helps more than learning techniques.

- The laws of boundaries are not about marriage as it should be; they are about marriage as it really is. Like the law of gravity, the laws of boundaries are always in force, whether or not we are aware of them. These laws lay the foundation of how responsibility works in life.

- **Law #1: The Law of Sowing and Reaping.** Our actions have consequences. When we do loving, responsible things, people draw close to us; when we are unloving or irresponsible, people withdraw from us.

- **Law #2: The Law of Responsibility.** We are responsible *to* each other, but not *for* each other. Spouses may help each other with the burdens of life (the financial, health, or emotional crises that come along), but, ultimately, each person must take care of his own daily responsibilities (including one's feelings, attitudes, values, and the handling of life's everyday difficulties).

- **Law #3: The Law of Power.** We don't have the power to change someone else, but we can influence them. We do have the power to confess, submit, and repent of our own hurtful ways and then be willing to change.

- **Law #4: The Law of Respect.** If we wish for others to respect our boundaries, it is our responsibility to respect theirs. We can't expect others to cherish our limits if we don't cherish theirs.

- **Law #5: The Law of Motivation.** We must be free to say no before we can wholeheartedly say yes. No one can actually love another if he feels he doesn't have a choice not to.

TIME TO INTERACT

Acknowledging the Laws in Your Life, Part 1

DIRECTIONS

We'll walk through these five laws together, first discussing them as a group. Then, as we finish discussing each law, I'll give you 2 minutes to start thinking about what that law means specifically for you in your marriage.

Law #1: The Law of Sowing and Reaping

1. When in your marriage have you not reaped the consequences you have sown—or in what ways are you avoiding them now?

2. When in your marriage has your spouse not reaped the consequences he or she has sown—or in what ways are you letting your spouse do so now?

3. In the first situation you identified, what consequences should you have been experiencing? In the second, what consequences should you have allowed or should you now allow your spouse to experience?

Law #2: The Law of Responsibility

1. In what area of marriage, if any, are you neglecting your responsibility? Are you, for instance, failing to love your spouse? In what ways are you violating the Golden Rule and not treating your mate as you yourself would want to be treated?

2. How, if at all, are you taking responsibility for your spouse's feelings, attitudes, values, or everyday difficulties? Or in what ways are you allowing your spouse to take responsibility for your feelings, attitudes, values, or everyday difficulties?

Law #3: The Law of Power

1. What about your spouse would you like to change? What about yourself (your attitude, your response, etc.) in regards to what you just identified about your spouse can you change—or, better yet, ask God to change?

2. What about yourself would you like to be able to change? Keep this in mind the next time you're confronted with a behavior in your spouse that you would like to change.

3. You don't have the power to change your spouse, but you do have the power to confess, submit, and repent of your own hurtful ways; to ask for God's help; to be willing to change; to identify ways you are contributing to your marriage problems; and to, over time, grow through the unhelpful ways you are dealing with those issues. Which one of these powers will you begin exercising this week? What specific step will you take?

Law #4: The Law of Respect

1. When did you last say no to your spouse? Describe the situation, focusing on how he or she reacted. On a scale of 1 to 10 (1 being the least respect), how respected did you feel? Why?

2. When did your spouse last say no to you? Again, describe the situation, focusing this time on how you reacted, internally as well as externally. On a scale of 1 to 10 (1 being the least respect), how respected did you feel? Why?

Law #5: The Law of Motivation

1. *Having* to do anything is a sign that someone is afraid. Fear of losing love, of a spouse's anger, of being alone, of being a "bad" person, of having to deal with guilt feelings, or of losing someone's approval are some of the fears that can motivate us to say yes when we want to say no. Which of these, if any, has interfered with your efforts to set or maintain boundaries in marriage?

2. What step(s) might you take to mature through those fears? Or who might be able to help you plan a course of action?

3. Learning to pay attention to your motives does not mean saying yes only when you feel like it or only when you want to do something—that is selfishness. When have you made the uncomfortable and painful choice to sacrifice for your mate? What motivated that choice?

4. When has your spouse made a significant sacrifice for you? What, if anything, did that action motivate you to do?

VIDEO SEGMENT
Five More Laws of Boundaries

- **Law #6: The Law of Evaluation.** It is our responsibility to evaluate the pain our boundaries cause others. Do they cause pain that leads to injury or do they cause pain that leads to growth?

- **Law #7: The Law of Proactivity.** This is a call to solve problems without blowing up, without waiting until we are reacting to others instead of intentionally living out our values.

- **Law #8: The Law of Envy.** This law addresses the most powerful obstacle to setting boundaries in marriage—envy. We will never get what we want if we focus outside of our boundaries on what others have.

- **Law #9: The Law of Activity.** It is our responsibility to take the initiative to solve our problems rather than being passive. Taking initiative increases one's chances to learn from mistakes.

- **Law #10: The Law of Exposure.** It is our responsibility to communicate our boundaries to each other. When boundaries are "exposed," two souls can be connected in the marriage.

- Applying these ten laws to your marriage can change the way you relate to each other. Remember, you can't break laws forever without consequences! These laws will help you shape your marriage into one based on God's principles of relationship.

TIME TO INTERACT

Acknowledging the Laws in Your Life, Part 2

DIRECTIONS

As we did earlier, we'll talk about each law, and then you'll have 2 minutes to begin thinking about what that law means specifically for you in your marriage.

Law #6: The Law of Evaluation

1. While it is unloving to set limits with a spouse to harm him or her, it can be just as unloving to avoid setting a limit with your spouse because you don't want him or her to be uncomfortable. Are you currently being unloving in either of these ways? What will you do to rectify the situation?

2. In what aspect of your marriage would your spouse's establishment of boundaries be wise—but you realize that he or she is failing to set boundaries out of the fear of hurting you or making you uncomfortable? What will you do or say to help ease your spouse's fear?

3. When has pain been a good friend to you? You might share that story with your spouse as you, in response to the preceding question, encourage him or her to set limits with you.

Law #7: The Law of Proactivity

1. Do you tend to wait to the point of blowing up before telling your spouse about something that is bothering you? Why have you chosen this path?

2. Does your spouse tend to wait to the point of blowing up before telling you about something that is bothering him or her? Why do you think your spouse has chosen this path? What might you do to encourage your spouse to be proactive?

3. What can you say to be proactive regarding a current issue in your marriage?

Law #8: The Law of Envy

1. On a scale of 1 to 10 with 1 being bright white and 10 being dark, forest green, how envious are you?

2. How envious is your spouse?

3. When, if at all, has the presence of envy in your marriage caused problems?

Law #9: The Law of Activity

1. Think about your marriage and whether one of you is the active spouse and the other the passive one. If you consider yourself the active spouse in your marriage, give two or three brief examples of your ability or tendency to take initiative. Also share a mistake or two you've made and what you've learned from them.

2. If you're the passive spouse, consider why you are passive. Is your active spouse dominating you? Are you too dependent on your spouse's initiative? Do you resent the power of the active spouse? Are you intimidated by your active spouse and unable to say no?

3. In what area of your marriage could you—and will you—take the initiative rather than merely wait for your spouse to act?

Law #10: The Law of Exposure

1. What boundaries are you not exposing to your spouse? Why are you making that choice?

2. Do you sense that your spouse is not exposing boundaries? What could you do to encourage openness?

3. Boundaries promote love and truth, and exposing our boundaries enables us to be fully connected to our spouse. Furthermore, exposure is the only way for healing and growth to take place. What step toward exposing some of your boundaries could you take this week?

Closing Prayer

Again, Lord, I find myself in awe of your design for marriage—and, as I read through these laws of boundaries in marriage, humbled by how far short of your standards I fall. I ask you to open my eyes to where the problems lie, to give me a heart that will love my spouse despite those problems, and to grant me the courage and wisdom to learn to act according to these laws of boundaries so that my marriage will indeed be informed by your principles. I pray in Jesus' name. Amen.

Boundary Building

1. Review the ten laws of boundaries. What action steps might help strengthen your marriage?

2. Spend some time each day this week praying for your spouse—for the ability to love him or her more, to appreciate what your mate brings to your marriage, and for creativity and energy to love him or her in ways that matter most.

3. Pray regularly, too, about the work God wants you to do in your life. Ask him to show you your shortcomings, to give you wisdom for what to do to make the right changes, and to keep you encouraged in the process.

Setting Boundaries with Yourself

OVERVIEW

In this session, you will

- Recognize that, no matter what the issue in your marriage, it is your responsibility to take the initiative to solve it.

- Identify your own character issues for which you need to set boundaries and consider boundaries you may need to set in regards to your spouse's character issues.

- Determine how, if at all, you attempt to control your spouse—and what steps to take to stop that controlling behavior.

VIDEO SEGMENT

What's a Spouse to Do?

- Lynn was tired of Tom always being late for dinner. Her reminding and nagging hadn't led to a change in his behavior.

- Lynn tried a new approach. First she apologized for her "negative attitude about dinnertime." She admitted to Tom that she had not been a nice person to come home to.

- In response, Tom confessed that he did want to avoid her resentment and anger.

- Lynn explained that she would be changing her attitude—and her actions. If Tom wasn't home for dinner with the family, he could reheat the plate she would leave for him in the refrigerator.

- Tom objected, and for the next few days he ate a lot of microwave dinners. Finally, he structured the end of his day to get home on time. Lynn's important family time became a reality.

TIME TO TALK

Whose Problem? My Problem!

DIRECTIONS

In groups of four or five, take 10 minutes to discuss the questions below. Remember to allow everyone in the group to share. We will review the questions with the large group after the exercise is over.

1. Describe each of the following situations in terms that show each problem to be the "good" spouse's problem:
   - A spouse's tendency to spend money
   - A spouse's habit of hiding behind a newspaper or in a novel
   - A spouse's habit of interrupting
   - A spouse who easily becomes angry
   - A spouse who emotionally withdraws from the relationship when conflict arises

2. Describe an ongoing problem in your relationship in terms that show it to be your problem, not your spouse's.

3. What does Lynn and Tom's story suggest about an action you could take to stop enabling your spouse?

VIDEO SEGMENT
Taking Ownership of Your Life

- Boundaries in marriage is not about changing, fixing, or making your spouse *do* anything. It's about bringing boundaries into the relationship so that the relationship is a place where both partners can grow.

- No matter what the issue in your marriage, it is your responsibility to take the initiative to solve it.

- When you cease to blame your spouse and own the problem as yours, you are then empowered to make changes to solve your problem.

- The "innocent" spouse needs to see what part, active or passive, he or she plays in the problem. In Matthew 7:5, Jesus called this the "plank" in our eyes. This plank may be some attitude or emotion we aren't aware of that encourages the problem to continue.

- We must acknowledge our own need for limits because it is our responsibility to submit to the same rules to which we want our partner to submit.

- We all want to find ways to say no to our spouse rather than to ourselves. Yet setting boundaries with ourselves may be the only hope for our marriage to develop a healthy set of boundaries. More specifically, in order to achieve a higher purpose, we must deny ourselves certain freedoms to say or do whatever we'd like.

- An important aspect of setting boundaries with ourselves is that of taking ownership of our lives. But it is much easier to blame and set boundaries with others who we think sorely need limits.

- It is our responsibility to submit ourselves to the same rules to which we want our partner to submit. It is the responsibility of both spouses to accept and respect the limits of the other; no one should play God, doing what he wants and expecting the other to comply.

TIME FOR THOUGHT
Establishing Boundaries for Myself

DIRECTIONS

Take 8 minutes on your own to think through and answer the four questions listed below.

1. More often than not, the first boundaries we set in marriage are with ourselves. In order to achieve a higher purpose, we deny ourselves certain freedoms to say or do whatever we'd like. What boundaries with yourself have you set, however consciously or unconsciously, to help make your marriage work? What boundaries do you think your spouse has set for him- or herself to help make your marriage work?

2. The reality of boundaries in marriage is that no matter what the issue in your marriage, it is your responsibility to take the initiative to solve it. Though you may share no blame in creating the problem, it is your responsibility to take some initiative in solving it. When, if ever, have you taken initiative to solve a problem you didn't cause? Be specific about why you did and the results of your efforts.

3. Taking ownership of our lives is not as easy as it sounds. It is much easier to blame and set boundaries with others who we think sorely need limits. For what are you blaming your spouse? Your answer may indicate areas where it is your responsibility to take ownership.

4. What boundaries are you trying to set with your spouse? Again, your answer may indicate a situation in which it is your responsibility to focus on yourself instead of your mate.

VIDEO SEGMENT
Setting Limits on Yourself

- We free our spouse to grow and change when we set limits on ourselves. You cannot make your spouse grow up—that matter is between him and God. But you can make it easier for him to experience the love and limits he needs in order to grow.

- There are two major areas in which it is our responsibility to set boundaries with ourselves in marriage. The first is our own character issues; the second is how we relate to our spouse's character issues.

- The highest calling of a spouse is the call to love, just as the highest calling of our faith is to love God and each other. Love means doing what is best for your spouse. Setting boundaries with your own character weaknesses is one of the most loving things you can do in your marriage.

- Some character issues on which we can set limits are: playing God instead of seeking him; denial, or not admitting the truth about who we are; withdrawal from relationship; irresponsibility; self-centeredness; and judgmentalism.

- Of all the aspects of ourselves for which we are responsible for setting limits, our tendency to control our spouse is probably the most crucial. If there is any surefire way to destroy trust and love, control is it. We must give our love freely.

- We attempt to control our spouse through guilt, anger, persistent assaults on his or her boundaries, and withholding love.

- Marriage has more to do with bringing yourself under the control of God and his principles than it does with controlling your spouse.

TIME TO ACT

DIRECTIONS

Take 12 minutes to read through the questions below and begin answering them. In your Boundary Building exercise for this week, you'll be asked to complete these questions at home.

Setting Boundaries

Although we can't change our destructive behaviors and attitudes automatically, we do have some power and choices. Below are some character issues on which we can set limits.

PLAYING GOD

By human nature, we try to play God instead of seeking him. In doing so, we miss the mark in loving, being responsible, and caring about the welfare of our spouse.

1. In what specific ways, if any, are you trying to play God in your marriage relationship?

2. What steps will you take to submit this part of yourself to God's authority? You might for example, ask God to help you lose your desire to play God or to help you practice more regularly and wholeheartedly the spiritual disciplines of worship, prayer, fellowship, and Scripture reading. As you stay in God's love, his presence in your life limits sin. Which of these steps will you focus on this week?

DENIAL

When we do not admit the truth about who we are, we give our spouse no one with whom to connect (1 John 1:8). What we deny about ourselves is absent from love.

1. What aspect of yourself, if any, are you denying? What failure, weakness, selfishness, or hurtfulness are you denying and rationalizing?

2. Ask God to prepare you and enable you to confess this tendency to your spouse—who most likely knows the truth anyway. At the same time, ask God to prepare your spouse to respond with compassion, support, and love. When will you confess what you've been denying? Set a specific time.

WITHDRAWAL FROM RELATIONSHIP

Failing to make and keep emotional connections is a serious character issue. Such emotional isolation withdraws the most basic part of us from the source of life: relatedness to God and others.

1. If you tend to withdraw, what do you think is behind that tendency? Do you struggle to trust? Do you fear that the relationship will control or hurt you? Does withdrawal help you feel safer and more protected? If you answered yes to any of these three questions, what might be the reason for your struggle to trust, your fear, or your sense of safety when you withdraw?

2. Which of the following steps will you take to help set boundaries with this tendency to withdraw from relationship:
   - Ask your spouse to let you know when he notices you pulling away and ask him how it affects him.
   - Discover why you withdraw. You could fear rejection, being controlled, or being judged. You could be punishing your spouse for hurting you.
   - Say no to your tendency to avoid relationships and expose yourself to others who can help you connect.

3. If your spouse tends to withdraw, what might you do to help her first recognize and then set boundaries with that tendency?

IRRESPONSIBILITY

Ever since the Fall, we have protested the reality that our lives are our problem and no one else's.

1. All of us desire either to have someone else take responsibility for us or to avoid the consequences of our actions. What evidence of this desire do you see in your own life? Do you, for instance, leave certain tasks undone at work or in your marriage? Do you argue when others say no? Be specific.

2. If you don't think you have a problem here, when will you ask your spouse in the off chance that you may?

3. If you have problems with responsibility, which of the following steps will you take to help set limits on this behavior?

- Submit yourself to safe people for accountability. They can help you see the problem when it occurs and then work with you to help you change.

- Accept both consequences and feedback for your problem. Ask others to stop enabling you (i.e., to leave for the party without you if you're late).

- Tell your spouse that his silence and/or nagging isn't helping you. Ask him to love you, but at the same time to provide limits for you when you don't set them on yourself.

SELF-CENTEREDNESS

Nothing is more natural than to think more of our own situation than another's. Thinking that the sun rises and sets only on us is one of the most destructive marriage-busting character issues. Marriage cannot be successfully navigated without our giving more of ourselves than we are comfortable giving.

1. In what ways, if any, are you trying to live as a single person in your marriage? What unrealistic and self-centered dreams (like wanting life to be put on hold the minute you return home from work), if any, are interfering with your marriage?

2. If you have problems with self-centeredness, which of the following steps will you take to help set limits on this behavior?

- Ask your spouse to tell you when he doesn't feel that things are mutual between you or when he thinks he has to constantly see reality your way.

- Learn to let go of the demand to be perfect or special. Instead, accept being loved for the real you, warts and all.

- Say no to the urge to be "good" and learn the skills of forgiveness and grief. Forgiveness and grief will help you accept the reality of who you are and who your spouse is.

JUDGMENTALISM

Many spouses struggle with judging, criticizing, and condemning others. They have difficulty accepting differences in others and see the differences as black and white.

1. Love cannot grow in a climate of fear (1 John 4:18). Are you the "judge" in your marriage? When do you find yourself hating both the sin and sinner?

2. If you tend to play the role of judge in your marriage, which of the following tasks will you take to help set limits on this behavior?
   - Ask for feedback on how your attitude hurts those you love. You may be surprised by how wounding you can be.
   - Become aware of your own attacking conscience. Learn to receive compassion and forgiveness from God and others for your own failings.
   - Develop compassion for the faults of others. Remember that we all are lost without God's help.

3. Setting limits on ourselves sometimes simply involves turning to a supportive relationship when feeling a troublesome emotion, behavior, or attitude, instead of acting on it. What supportive relationship can you turn to—or where could you go to begin developing that kind of relationship?

Recognizing Our Attempts to Control

Control comes in many different flavors. Here are some ways spouses try to control each other.

GUILT

Guilt messages are intended to make our spouse feel responsible for our welfare. Guilt controls by creating the impression that our spouse's freedom injures us. By exercising freedom and choosing differently than what we would want, we wrongly think that our spouse is being unloving.

1. When, if at all, was the most recent time you communicated a guilt message to your spouse? What method, such as a wounded silence or an "If you really loved me" or "How could you be so selfish?" statement, did you use? What would have been a healthier way to communicate your thoughts and feelings?

2. When, if at all, was the most recent time your spouse communicated a guilt message to you? What means did he or she use? How did you respond—and how would you have liked to respond?

ANGER

Often, when one spouse wants something the other doesn't, the disappointed mate will become angry. Anger is our basic protest against the fact that we are not God and that we cannot control reality.

1. Is anger a tool you use to attempt to control your spouse? If so, are you direct (throwing tantrums) or covert (being

passive-aggressive or sarcastic)? What threat(s) do you make? Why do you think you choose this behavior? What actions would be healthier?

2. Does your spouse tend to use anger in an attempt to control you? If so, is he or she direct, throwing tantrums, or covert, being passive-aggressive or sarcastic? What threat(s) does he or she make? How do you respond—and how would you like to respond—to this anger?

PERSISTENT ASSAULTS ON THE SPOUSE'S BOUNDARIES

One person will say no, then the spouse will make attempt after attempt to change the other's mind by arguing, wheedling, and pleading until the other is worn down.

1. Do you tend to be like a strong-willed door-to-door salesperson when your spouse says no to you? What boundaries are you most unwilling to accept? Give an example. Why won't you respect his or her no and live with the boundary being set?

2. Does your spouse tend to be like a strong-willed door-to-door salesperson when you say no? What boundaries does he or she seem most unwilling to accept? Give an example. What might be a healthy way of dealing with your spouse's arguing, wheedling, and pleading?

WITHHOLDING LOVE

Of all the ways we attempt to control, withholding love may be the most powerful. When one spouse disagrees, the other disconnects emotionally until the spouse changes to suit her.

1. Are you sometimes guilty as charged? When did you last resort to this means of control? What might have been a healthier way to deal with the situation?

2. Does your spouse ever withhold love in an attempt to control you? What might you do to make this attempt to control you ineffective?

Closing Prayer

Again, Lord God, I'm humbled by how much growing I have ahead of me as well as by the fact that boundaries are basically an issue between you and me. In light of that fact, I pray that you will show me where it is my responsibility to set boundaries with myself; where it is my responsibility to take ownership of my heart, my love, my time, and my talent; where it is my responsibility to stop blaming; and where it is my responsibility to be sure I'm living by the same rules I want my spouse to live by. Help me to set boundaries on myself and to have the courage, energy, and insight to do the work on those aspects of my character that need work. I submit to you this process of growth. I ask you to not only guide me but also to bless my efforts. Make me more like Christ, more loving and more lovable, a person who lives the Golden Rule he taught. In his name I pray. Amen.

Boundary Building

1. Finish answering the questions for the Setting Boundaries exercise. Choose one specific area to focus on this week.

2. Finish answering the questions for the Recognizing Our Attempts to Control exercise. In your prayers for your marriage this week, include your attempts to control your spouse.

3. In light of what you learned about yourself in the Recognizing Our Attempts to Control exercise, ask the Lord to help you make the changes in yourself that you want to make.

Values One and Two: Love of God and Love of Spouse

OVERVIEW

In this session, you will

- Look at the first two of six values that, if a couple holds them up high, esteems them, and pursues them as a couple, will help them build their relationship on solid ground and cause it to grow in the direction God intends.

- Learn why loving God—the first value—must be the top priority in a marriage.

- Discover what loving your spouse "as yourself"— the second value—means in marriage.

VIDEO SEGMENT
Value One: Love of God

- Ultimately, in a relationship, what you value is what you will have. If you value something in a relationship, you will not tolerate anything that destroys this value, and you will also seek to make sure it is present and growing. What you value happens, and what you don't value will be absent.

- Jesus said that the greatest commandment is to love God with every ounce of yourself: "with all your heart and with all your soul and with all your mind and with all your strength" (Mark 12:30). When loving God like that is our orienting principle in life, we are always adjusting to what he requires from us.

- When things get tough in a marriage and some change is required from us, we might not want to do it. But if we know that it is God with whom we ultimately have to deal, we submit to this reality and to his higher calling to us to grow. In the end, the relationship wins.

- The once-hopeless couple I (Dr. Cloud) talked about loved God enough to do what God asked of them, and they grew to love each other as a result. The love that they now have for each other is a fruit of loving God.

- Loving God must be first priority because he empowers us to change, he tells us how to change, and, most of all, he becomes the one that keeps us from being ultimately in charge. If we try to be in charge, we will do marriage our way, and then our own limitations become the limitations of the relationship as well. We all need someone bigger to answer to so we will make the changes we are responsible for making.

TIME TO TALK
Some Defining Values

DIRECTIONS

In groups of four or five, discuss the questions listed below, giving each member of the group a chance to contribute. You will have 10 minutes to complete this exercise.

1. What bad things are not present in your marriage because of the values that you—and your spouse—hold?

2. What good things are present in your marriage and do you seek to have in your marriage because of the values that you—and your spouse—hold?

3. Think about the once-hopeless couple from the video. What role did their submission to God play in building a stronger marriage?

TIME FOR THOUGHT
Loving God

DIRECTIONS

The questions below will help you think more specifically about how loving God can be important in your relationship with your spouse. Take 7 minutes now on your own to complete these questions.

1. What, if any, current issue in your marriage (judgmentalism, sarcasm, not wanting to listen, wanting to avoid conflict, bitterness and fears, blame, or something else) might God be calling you to change? Be specific about that change and why you might be hesitant to work on changing.

2. What behaviors, attitudes, habits, etc. is God calling you to submit to him so that, by the power of his Spirit, he can change you?

3. Loving God must be our first priority because he empowers us to change, he tells us how to change, and he keeps us from being ultimately in charge. If we try to be in charge, we will do marriage our way, and then our own limitations become the limitations of the relationship. In what aspects of your marriage are you trying to be in charge? How, if at all, are your ways in these areas contradictory to God's ways? Which of your limitations are limiting your marriage?

4. For what specific action, statement, effort, or attitude in regards to his or her love of God can you affirm your spouse? Do so!

VIDEO SEGMENT

Value Two: Love of Spouse

- When we don't see what we love about our spouse, or when our love disappears, we need to rely on the love that builds a marriage. That kind of love is the kind of love God has for us. It is called "agape."

- Agape love seeks the welfare of the other. It is love that has nothing to do with how someone is gratifying us at the moment. Instead, it has to do with what is good for the other. In short, agape is concerned with the good of the other person.

- In the second greatest commandment, Jesus said, "Love your neighbor as yourself." In marriage, loving someone as yourself means, first, to so deeply identify with your spouse that you think about and even feel the effects of your own behavior on your spouse. This identifying with another's experience is called empathy. Empathy empowers you to seek the best for the other person because it puts you in touch with her life and how it feels to be her, especially on the other end of a relationship with you.

- Second, loving your spouse as yourself means you think of making your spouse's life better. When you feel the other person's need as your own (empathy) and you sacrifice to meet it, you also find joy in the happiness and fulfillment that she finds.

- Third—and this is often the most difficult aspect of loving your spouse as yourself—loving your spouse as yourself means you want the best for your spouse even when your spouse can't see what that is.

- In addition to being based in empathy, agape love is based in commitment. To commit to someone means that you will stay, even when things get difficult. In marriage, commitment provides the time, structure, and security needed for growth and change to take place. Commitment keeps the patient on the table until the surgery is finished.

- Commitment both provides the security necessary for growth and drives the need for growth and resolution.

- As important as commitment in a marriage is the element of action. Love is not just a feeling or an attachment to a person, it is an expression of that attachment. True love will not allow itself to go cold. When love begins to cool, there is a call to action. As Jesus says of our relationship to God, "do the things you did at first" (Revelation 2:5). The need for action in a love relationship never goes away.

TIME FOR THOUGHT
Loving Your Mate

DIRECTIONS

The questions listed below will help you think more specifically about what God wants you to do in terms of loving your spouse. You'll have 7 minutes on your own to answer them.

1. Loving your spouse as yourself means so deeply identifying with your spouse that you feel the effects of your own behavior on your spouse. Think back over your interactions with your spouse this past week.

   - When were you acting in word and deed solely to please yourself?

   - How did your spouse react to those moments you just listed?

   - What would it have been like in those moments to be on the other end of a relationship with you?

2. Loving your spouse as yourself means you think about how to make your spouse's life better.

   - What is your spouse's current situation? What stresses is he or she under? What responsibilities, worries, or hurts is he or she carrying? What decisions, frustrations, or transitions is he or she facing?

- What would you want if you were in your spouse's situation, the situation you just described? What will you do to give that to your spouse?

3. Loving your spouse as yourself means you want the best for your spouse even when your spouse can't see what that is.

   - When, if ever, have you had the opportunity to love your spouse in this way? What did you do—or what do you wish you had done?

   - When, if ever, has your spouse had the opportunity to love you in this way? Describe the situation and the growth that occurred if your spouse acted courageously and loved boldly.

   - What current opportunity, if any, do you have to love your spouse in a way that your spouse may not initially experience as love? What does this discussion of love motivate you to do?

4. For what specific action, statement, effort, or attitude in regard to loving you can you affirm your spouse? Do so!

TIME TO INTERACT

The Greatest of These Is Love

Love is patient, love is kind. It does not envy, it does not boast, it is not proud. It is not rude, it is not self-seeking, it is not easily angered, it keeps no record of wrongs. Love does not delight in evil but rejoices with the truth. It always protects, always trusts, always hopes, always perseveres. Love never fails (1 Corinthians 13:4–8).

1. Which aspect(s) of love listed here are especially important in marriage? Why?

2. What past experiences in your marriage does this list of love's attributes affirm the value of? What growth has resulted because you and your spouse have loved each other in one of the ways described here?

3. If you make love the highest value in your marriage, it is likely to return the commitment you make to it. When have you seen your efforts to love your spouse rewarded? Be specific.

4. What dimension(s) of love listed in 1 Corinthians 13:4–8 did you need to be reminded of right now? Make that area of growth a topic of prayer this week, perhaps a prayer of confession as well as supplication.

Closing Prayer

Father God, help me to love you enough to make the changes that you want me to make and to stand strong in my commitment to do whatever you ask of me in this process of growing in character and strengthening my marriage. May your love truly be the orienting principle in all I do in and for my marriage.

And, Father, teach me how to love my spouse with agape love. Help me to deeply identify with my mate, to think about the effects of my behavior on him or her, and to get out of the self-centeredness of just acting to please myself. Enable me to work on making my spouse's life better, to regularly ask myself, "What would I like if I were in my spouse's situation?" And, when appropriate, help me to love my spouse as myself by wanting the best for him even when he can't see what that is.

Besides teaching me empathy, grant me the grace to be true to my covenant commitment to my mate. Show me— guide me in—the actions which it is my responsibility to take in order to strengthen my marriage. Fill me with your love so that I can place my mate above my own selfish needs and desires, so that I can weather the hurts and storms that come with marriage. I pray in Jesus' name. Amen.

Boundary Building

1. If you haven't already, take the action steps (repeated below) that you identified at the end of the two Time for Thought exercises:

    • For what specific action, statement, effort, or attitude in regards to his or her love of God can you affirm your spouse? Do so!

- For what specific action, statement, effort, or attitude in regard to loving you can you affirm your spouse? Do so!

2. Take some time this week to work through the following "Commitment Counts" questions.

COMMITMENT COUNTS

Commitment is key to marriage. To commit to someone means that you will be there and that you will stay even when things get difficult.

- When have you and your spouse stayed in the marriage—emotionally as well as physically—and worked through a difficult time? What kept you from leaving? What rewards came from hanging in there and going through the necessary changes?

- What current challenge is calling for you to stand on the commitment you made to your spouse?

- What can and will you do to let your mate know you are committed to him or her and that you aren't going to leave?

- When has the fact that you're in your marriage for the long-term compelled you to deal with an issue? Explain what happened and how your commitment to the marriage kept you working.

- If you're going to be with someone for the long-term, it's best to work things out. Such commitment often drives one toward resolution. What issue in your marriage that you've been ignoring, hoping it would go away, does this statement encourage you to address?

3. Work through the following "Ready, Set, Go!" action questions during the week.

READY, SET, GO!

As James observed long ago, faith without action is dead (James 2:17). Love is not just a feeling or an attachment to a person, it is an expression of that attachment. Yet the more familiar they are with someone, the lazier people get.

- In the early days of your courtship and marriage, what actions did you take to express your love to your spouse?

- In what ways have you gotten lazy? Which of the actions you just listed will you once again start doing, beginning this week?

- True love will not allow itself to go cold. When it begins to cool, there is a call to action, a call to rekindle the flame. What sign(s) are you aware of that your love for your spouse needs some rekindling?

- What steps will you take to rekindle your love, to not allow your love for your spouse to grow cool?

Values Three and Four: Honesty and Faithfulness

OVERVIEW

In this session, you will

- Consider how harmful deception is in a relationship and, therefore, how crucial total honesty is.
- Determine what fears, if any, keep you from being totally honest.
- Define faithfulness to mean far more than "able to be trusted in the area of sexual relations."

VIDEO SEGMENT

Avoiding the Unforgivable Relational Sin

- Deception damages a relationship. The act of lying is much more damaging than the things being lied about, because lying undermines the knowing of one another and the connection itself.

- Anything, large or small, is forgivable and able to be worked through in a relationship—except deception. Deception is the one thing that cannot be worked through because it denies the problem. It is the one unforgivable sin of a relationship because it makes forgiveness unattainable. (Of course, if it is confessed, deception is forgivable. But no problem can be worked through if it is denied.)

- We believe in total honesty. But honesty must go along with the other values (love, commitment to one's spouse, commitment to holiness, forgiveness) we have discussed.

- If there are barriers to honesty, knowing one another intimately is ruled out and falsehood takes over. Couples often live out years of falsehood trying to protect and save a relationship, all the while destroying any chance of real relationship.

- We can't stress enough the importance of being able to share with each other your deepest feelings, needs, hurts, desires, failures, or whatever else is in your soul. Yet couples often find it difficult to be honest about feelings, disappointments, desires, likes and dislikes, hurts, anger and hatred, sex, sins, failure, and needs and vulnerabilities.

- Most of the time, in otherwise good marriages, deception takes place for "defensive" reasons. In other words, the dishonest spouse is often lying not for evil reasons, but to protect himself.

- Fears drive the deception. For spouses to tell the whole truth, they must deal with their fears first—fear of real closeness and being known; fear of abandonment and loss of love if they are known; fear of being controlled and possessed if they are known; fear of being seen as "bad" or not good enough; and fear of their own desires, needs, and feelings.

- A strong relationship requires a commitment to each other of total honesty. But remember that honesty must be accompanied by enough grace to hear and deal with the truth it brings.

TIME TO TALK

Total Commitment to Total Honesty

DIRECTIONS

Now it's time to talk to your spouse. Dr. Townsend and Dr. Cloud have outlined a six-point commitment to honesty.

Take 5 minutes to answer the "On Your Own" questions listed below. Then turn to your spouse and take 10 minutes to go through the six-point commitment and discuss the questions listed under "With Your Spouse."

ON YOUR OWN

1. In which of the following areas do you find it difficult to be honest with your spouse?

> Feelings
> Disappointments
> Desires, likes, and dislikes
> Hurts
> Anger and hatred
> Sex
> Sins
> Failure
> Needs and vulnerabilities

2. Now consider carefully the areas you marked. What feelings, needs, hurts, desires, failures, or secrets of your soul would you like to be able to share with your spouse?

    • What is keeping you from doing so?

- What will you do to overcome those barriers or your own resistance?

3. What role could the development or strengthening of healthy boundaries play in overcoming those barriers to honesty?

WITH YOUR SPOUSE

Six-Point Commitment

1. Have enough grace to tell the truth. Promise that you will never punish your spouse for being honest.

2. Give each other free rein to question and check out things with each other. Don't be offended by your spouse's need to understand some facts that don't add up.

3. Police each other when you see your spouse not being totally honest. Your policing can be harmless and light-handed, but hold your spouse to the truth.

4. Become a partner in your spouse's life to heal the underlying fears of being honest.

5. Take responsibility for your own dishonesty and its underlying fears, and make a commitment to resolve them.

6. Use discernment. While total honesty is ideal, every relationship is not ready for total knowing and being known. Use wisdom to know what your relationship can handle and what it is not ready for.

1. Which of these six points are already in place in your marriage?

2. Which of these six points would you like to add to or further develop? What barriers to this growth do you face? What will you do to overcome those barriers? Be specific.

> If you're working through this book on your own, make a date with your spouse to talk about honesty in your marriage and review these six points. (In fact, you might even want to make a series of dates—one date per value!)

VIDEO SEGMENT
Being Faithful No Matter What

- Trust. Confidence. Assuredness. Conviction. Fidelity. Truth. Certainty. Permanence. Rest. All of these words hint at what faithfulness is. The idea of faithfulness becomes even clearer when you put these words into the context of marriage: Trust each other. Have confidence in each other. Be assured of each other's character and dependability. Be convicted of your ability to trust each other. Be certain of each other's fidelity. Be true to one another. Be certain of one another. Be permanent to each other. Rest in each other.

- A faithful spouse is one who can be trusted, depended upon, and believed in, and one in whom you can rest.

- Our notion of faithfulness in marriage is too often shallow. We generally think of it only in the physical realm. Yet, in many marriages spouses are physically faithful but not emotionally faithful. They are faithful with their bodies but not with their hearts. The partners can't depend on each other in the ways listed above. There is little trust, little certainty, little safety.

- Faithfulness means to be trusted in all areas, not just the sexual—in matters of the heart as well as those of the body.

- Being faithful to your spouse means that you can be depended upon to do what you have promised, to follow through on what your spouse has entrusted to you. It means that your spouse can be certain you will deliver on what you have promised. This could mean being sexually faithful, but it could also mean doing chores faithfully. It could mean staying within the monthly budget and coming home when you say you will. It could mean sharing without fear of reprisal or condemnation.

- One of the words the Bible uses for trust (the Hebrew word *batach*) means to be so confident that you can be "care-less." In other words, you don't have to worry.

- An affair of the heart means taking aspects of yourself and intentionally keeping them away from the marriage. Now this does not mean that you cannot have deep, sustaining, healing, and supportive emotional relationships with other people. We strongly believe in the power of friends to heal, sustain, and support.

- An affair of the heart means taking aspects of yourself and intentionally keeping them away from your marriage (e.g., using other things in life—not only a relationship, but also work, a hobby, or an addiction—to avoid your spouse). Some part of you avoids the relationship. This dynamic is about deliberately splitting yourself into two people, one of whom is not connected to the marriage.

- Many times one of the partners will justify unfaithfulness by the other's behavior by saying, "If she hadn't been so critical. . ." or "If he'd been meeting my needs." But such reasoning couldn't be farther from the truth. An act of unfaithfulness is something that one person does, not two.

- Make a commitment to each other that you will not allow anything to come between you. You will be trustworthy. You will be dependable. You will be sexually and emotionally faithful.

Time to Talk

How Great Is Your Faithfulness?

DIRECTIONS

Take 10 minutes alone to consider the questions on faithfulness found below under "On Your Own." Then turn to your spouse and take 5 minutes to discuss the questions on faithfulness found under "With Your Spouse."

ON YOUR OWN

1. Trust. Confidence. Assuredness. Conviction. Fidelity. Truth. Certainty. Permanence. Rest. These words hint at what faithfulness is. Are you a faithful spouse? On what points do you feel weak?

2. Can your spouse depend on you to deliver what you promise? To do chores faithfully as well as be sexually faithful? To stay within the monthly budget as well as to come home when you say you will? To hear his or her heart without reprisal or condemnation?

    *   Which of these points—or which other behaviors where you are currently less than faithful—is it your responsibility to work on?

3. What aspects of yourself (if any) are you keeping away from your marriage? Consider what things you may be using to

avoid your spouse. Is work, a hobby, or an addiction interfering? If you're not sure, your spouse may offer confirmation.

- If something is interfering in your marriage, why are you letting it—and what will you do to make the necessary changes?

WITH YOUR SPOUSE

1. Affirm your spouse for the faithfulness you noticed as you worked on the preceding questions.

2. On what points—trust, confidence, assuredness, conviction, fidelity, truth, certainty, permanence, rest—can you affirm your spouse's faithfulness? Affirm him or her for being faithful in those ways.

3. Which of the following can you depend on your spouse to do?
   - Deliver on promises
   - Do chores faithfully
   - Be sexually faithful
   - Stay within the monthly budget
   - Come home when promised
   - Hear your heart without reprisal or condemnation

4. Which of the points listed above can your spouse depend on you to do? What steps will you take to become more faithful in the remaining areas?

Closing Prayer

Almighty God, as you continue to work in my life, make me a person of truth in matters large and small, in deeds as well as words. May the presence of your perfect love in my marriage help cast out any fear I have about being totally honest with my mate. Lord, I ask you to make me a person who can hear the truth my spouse speaks so that our marriage will indeed—with your blessing—be a source of life to both of us. Teach me also to be faithful to my spouse—emotionally as well as physically—even when I am feeling disappointed, hurt, or unloved. And help me to "remain faithful until the end." Amen.

Boundary Building

1. If you haven't already, affirm your spouse for the honesty and faithfulness you see in him or her. If you have, find another reason for this kind of affirmation.

   • For what specific action, statement, effort, or attitude in regards to honesty can you affirm your spouse?

- For what action, statement, effort, or attitude in regards to faithfulness can you affirm your spouse?

2. What, if anything, about how you feel in your marriage and your desires for your marriage have you not yet been able to share with your spouse? How is your quietness on these matters inhibiting the development of deeper intimacy?

3. Which of the common fears listed below do you experience? What will you do to work through those fears? (The books *Changes That Heal* and *Hiding from Love* may help.)

   - Fears of real closeness and being known
   - Fears of abandonment and loss of love if you are known
   - Fears of being controlled and possessed if you are known
   - Fears of being seen as "bad" or not good enough if some part of you is known
   - Fears of your own desires, needs, and feelings

4. Talk with your mate about how honesty can become the bedrock of all that you do together. Then determine how to protect your marriage against deception as well as how to build in honesty.

5. God does not become unfaithful if we do not love him correctly. He remains faithful no matter what we do. Marriage requires this as well. Do not let your spouse's failures in love be an excuse for your unfaithfulness.

- When has your spouse been faithful to you despite your failures in love?

- What opportunities have you had—or what opportunity do you currently have—to be faithful to your spouse despite his or her failures in love? If the situation is a current one, ask God to enable you to be faithful.

Values Five and Six: Compassion and Forgiveness, and Holiness

OVERVIEW

In this session, you will

- Recognize what tenderheartedness and compassion mean in a marriage of two imperfect beings who sin and disappoint one another.

- Broaden your definition of holiness to mean being reality-oriented.

- See how the value of holiness means the presence of the following in relationships:

  — Confession and ownership of the problems by each individual
  — A relentless drive toward growth and development
  — A giving up of everything that gets in the way of love
  — A surrendering of everything that gets in the way of truth
  — A purity of heart where nothing toxic is allowed to grow

VIDEO SEGMENT

Clothe Yourself with Compassion

- The person you love the most and to whom you have committed your life is an imperfect being. This person is guaranteed to hurt you and fail you in many ways, some serious and some not.

- What do you do when your spouse fails you in some way or is less than you wish him to be?

- The Bible says that "love covers over a multitude of sins" (1 Peter 4:8). Nothing in a relationship has to permanently destroy a relationship if forgiveness is in the picture. No failure is larger than grace. No hurt exists that love cannot heal. For all of these miracles to take place, however, there must be compassion and tenderheartedness.

- Hardness of heart, much more than failure, is the true relationship killer. That is why the Bible places such a high value on tenderheartedness.

- Tenderheartedness consists of an identification with sin and failure; an identification with weakness; a willingness to become vulnerable again; and a willingness to repent.

- Compassion, tenderheartedness, and forgiveness ensure that imperfect people can experience love and relationship for a long time. So, as Paul says in the Bible, clothe yourselves with the qualities of compassion, kindness, humility, gentleness, and patience.

TIME TO TALK

Becoming Tenderhearted

DIRECTIONS

The questions below will help you think more carefully about how you respond to your spouse's failures and how you want to be able to respond. You will have 15 minutes to read through all these questions and discuss those in boldface type.

As stated in the video segment, hardness of heart, much more than failure, is the true relationship killer (see Matthew 19:8). The Bible places a high value on tenderheartedness because its opposite—hardheartedness—destroys relationships. But what is tenderheartedness, and are you a tenderhearted spouse? Tenderheartedness consists of:

An identification with sin and failure. Make sure you have an attitude of humility toward your spouse's failure. If you are very familiar with your own sins, you will have a lot more grace for your spouse's.

1. Do you have a familiarity with your own sins that fosters in you an attitude of humility toward your spouse's failures? List some of your own sins that keep you humble.

2. **What can a person do to become familiar with his or her own sins?**

3. What will you do to become familiar—or more familiar—with your own sins? And what will you do to repent of them and change?

An identification with weakness. If you are staying away from your own hurts and vulnerabilities, you will not be able to identify with the hurts of your spouse either. Deal with your own pains and hurts and you will have more empathy for your spouse, identifying with your spouse's weakness or inability as if it were your own.

1. **Why does dealing with one's own pains, hurts, and vulnerabilities make someone more compassionate and empathic? Give an example from your own life or from the life of someone you know.**

2. What pains and hurts have you been trying to ignore? What might you do to deal with them—or to begin to figure out how to deal with them?

A willingness to become vulnerable again. Sometimes people build up protectiveness from childhood. But if your spouse has hurt you and is truly repentant and can be trusted, dare to open up and be vulnerable again. That is what God does with us.

1. **Why do people build walls to protect themselves?**

2. Why have you (if you have) built a wall to protect yourself?

3. **What can those people who build walls do to remove them?**

4. What could you to do to start taking that wall down—or to begin to figure out how to take it down?

A willingness to repent. Forgiveness and tenderheartedness come from the injured party. But for it to be useful for the future of the relationship, the person who failed must own his failure and show a true change of heart.

1. When you fail, in what way do you own that failure and show a true change of heart and resulting change of behavior? Give a recent example.

2. **What are some reasons why people don't own their failure?**

3. Is it hard for you to own your failure? Why or why not? What might you do to soften your heart so that genuine repentance comes more easily to you?

What do your answers to these four areas show you about yourself?

What steps can you take toward being more compassionate and forgiving? Be sure to involve God in this heart-changing process.

VIDEO SEGMENT

Get Holy!

- To be holy means to be pure and blameless. The Bible pictures holiness as not just being religious, but also being reality-oriented.

- Because God is holy, his reality is ultimate reality. To the extent that we are not holy, we are farther away from the reality of life itself. God is life and ultimate reality, so our unholiness is a movement away from the ultimate reality of life.

- If every marriage placed value on holiness, the following would be present in those relationships:

  — Confession and ownership of the problems by each individual
  — A relentless drive toward growth and development
  — A giving up of everything that gets in the way of love
  — A surrendering of everything that gets in the way of truth
  — A purity of heart where nothing toxic is allowed to grow

- Pursuing holiness means becoming whole, trustworthy, honest, faithful, and loving.

TIME TO TALK

An (Ultimate) Reality Check

DIRECTIONS

The questions below will encourage you to look closely at yourself and consider how holy you are. You will have 15 minutes to discuss the questions below.

Dr. Townsend and Dr. Cloud maintain that, if every marriage placed value on holiness, these five things would be present:

- Confession and ownership of the problems in each individual
- A relentless drive toward growth and development
- A giving up of everything that gets in the way of love
- A surrendering of everything that gets in the way of truth
- A purity of heart where nothing toxic is allowed to grow

1. Review the definition of "holiness" and then look again at the five traits listed above.

   - What is the connection between confession and holiness? Between taking ownership and holiness?

   - Why does a drive toward growth and development foster the development of holiness in one's character and in one's marriage?

   - What are some things that get in the way of love? What does giving them up involve? Be specific and remember that these questions are asked in a discussion of holiness.

- What gets in the way of truth in a marriage relationship? What would surrendering these roadblocks involve?

- What toxic things can grow in a heart? What can people do to prune the garden of such weeds?

- What does this checklist suggest about what people can do to grow in holiness? Be specific.

2. On a scale of 1 to 10 (1 standing for "We're at square one!" and 10 standing for "We've arrived at God's standard!") to what degree are these five traits present, in your marriage? Determine which areas invite the most growth. Give specific evidence of each trait's presence in your marriage.

3. What does this checklist and your answer to the preceding question suggest about what you can do to develop holiness in yourself and therefore in your marriage? Be specific about

action steps you can take. Then choose one step to take this week. Ask your spouse to pray for you and perhaps even hold you accountable as you move toward becoming more holy—as you move toward God and his ultimate and life-giving reality.

Closing Prayer

Loving and forgiving God, you call me to clothe myself with compassion, tenderheartedness, and forgiveness. I know that it is my responsibility to choose to be compassionate, tender, and forgiving with my spouse. But I also know that, in my sin, I can't simply will myself to be that way. I ask that you would be at work in me to make my compassion, tenderheartedness, and forgiveness a reflection of yours. Also, as I consider who you want me to be, I ask you to keep my heart soft toward you. Keep me submitting to you. May I be clay in your hands so I can be trustworthy, honest, faithful, and loving; so that I may be holy as you are holy. I pray in the name of your holy Son. Amen.

Boundary Building

1. Let your mate know how much you appreciate the compassion and forgiveness as well as the holiness you see in him or her.

   • For what specific action, statement, effort, or attitude in regards to compassion and forgiveness can you affirm your spouse? Do so!

   • For what specific action, statement, effort, or attitude in regards to holiness can you affirm your spouse? Do so!

2. The Bible says, "Love covers over a multitude of sins"
   (1 Peter 4:8).What can you do when your spouse fails you
   in some way or is less than you wish for him to be?

   • What are some of your sins that your spouse's love has
     covered?

   • What sins of your spouse could you choose to cover
     with love?

   • Dr. Cloud said, "Nothing in a relationship has to per-
     manently destroy that relationship if forgiveness is in
     the picture. No failure is larger than grace. No hurt
     exists that love cannot heal." Into what situation in
     your life or your marriage do these words speak hope?
     Make that situation a focus of your prayers this week.

3. Consider again Kate and David's relationship, which Dr.
   Cloud described in the "Get Holy!" video segment. Until
   holiness was important to David apart from what Kate
   wanted from him, he was not truly holy.

- On a scale of 1 to 10 (1 being "Why does it even matter?" and 10 being "Hungering for holiness like a starving man longs for food"), how motivated are you to be holy?

- What might result in your person as well as in your marriage if you wholeheartedly pursued holiness for the sake of holiness? Paint a picture, no matter how idealistic it sounds, and remember that God can do far more than we ask or imagine (Ephesians 3:20).

4. Think again about the action steps you outlined in the An (Ultimate) Reality Check exercise. What are you doing to pursue holiness—and what could you be doing? Be specific about your program and/or your plan.

Resolving Conflict in Marriage

OVERVIEW

In this session, you will

- See that conflict is not all the same and that the rules are different for different kinds of conflict. In most conflicts, though, there is not a right or wrong.

- Examine six common marital conflicts:
  - Conflict #1: The Sin of One Spouse
  - Conflict #2: The Immaturity or Brokenness of One Person
  - Conflict #3: Hurt Feelings That Are No One's Fault
  - Conflict #4: Conflicting Desires
  - Conflict #5: Desires of One Person Versus the Needs of the Relationship
  - Conflict #6: Known Versus Unknown Problems

- Review the Bible's path for resolving all kinds of conflicts: observation; confrontation; ownership, grief, and apology; repentance; involvement in the process; reexamination. Don't be afraid of conflict. Go through it lovingly, and chances are you will find more intimacy with your mate on the other side.

VIDEO SEGMENT
Those Unavoidable Sparks

- Conflict is not all the same. And the rules are different for different kinds of conflict. In most conflicts, though, there is not a right or wrong.

- **Conflict #1: The Sin of One Spouse.** One spouse has sinned against the other. The sin could be sexual sin, angry outbursts, loss of self-control, impatience, critical attitudes, judgmentalism, out-of-control spending of the family money (thievery), lying or deception, substance abuse, controlling behavior, emotionally injurious behavior (name calling or belittling), misuse of power, pride, selfishness, greed, jealousy, envy, or conceit.

- **Conflict #2: The Immaturity or Brokenness of One Person.** When immaturity or brokenness surfaces, face that reality and deal with it. Equality and mutuality—instead of an attitude of superiority—can solve a lot of problems if you are working as a team.

- **Conflict #3: Hurt Feelings That Are No One's Fault.** Marriage is a place where old hurts inevitably get stepped on. But old hurts can heal as you respond differently to your spouse than he has been responded to in his "past life." Though you can't "fix" your spouse, you can become a healing agent, with empathy, understanding, non-defensiveness, and care.

- **Conflict #4: Conflicting Desires.** Normally, two people develop a pattern of give and take, and differences get negotiated. But sometimes there is a stalemate. Instead of fighting for your own way, give in to the preference of your spouse as a learning and stretching experience. Your marriage relationship can grow you and expand you if you let it.

- **Conflict #5: Desires of One Person Versus the Needs of the Relationship.** Make sure that the marriage gets served first. Also, over the long haul, see that the marriage goes on the back burner at times for each member and that each member has learned that the marriage is more important than his or her individual wants.

- **Conflict #6: Known Versus Unknown Problems.** Your spouse may know more about you than you do. Learn what your spouse knows about you and then work together to solve the problem. Furthermore, you may both become aware of problems that you hadn't known about before.

TIME TO TALK

What's Really Going On Here?

DIRECTIONS

Split into groups of six and review the six conflicts from the video segment on pages 100 and 101. Each group will be assigned a scenario and will have 4 minutes to decide what conflict it most closely represents. If time allows, answer the three questions that follow the scenarios.

SCENARIO #1

"Sex was always so mechanical for her. She never said no to me—and I always had to be the one to initiate—but it's as if she checked out whenever we got close. About two years into our marriage, she opened up about the incest she had experienced as a child."

Conflict #_____

SCENARIO #2

"She always seems to be on the phone when I'm home. It's not that I expect a candlelight dinner, the red-carpet treatment, and her undivided attention every moment I'm under the roof. But, for whatever reason, I'm really bugged by the phone thing. I guess I want more than the nod, half-smile, and 'I'll-just-be-a-minute' sign. She doesn't even skip a beat in her conversation… But maybe she's not even aware of the pattern."

Conflict #_____

SCENARIO #3

"Lunch at 11:15. I remembered that as easily as I remember my telephone number! But 11:15 came and went, and he didn't show up. I called him on my cell phone, but no one answered at his office. So I had a salad by myself. I was more than a little miffed, and I got angrier as the afternoon wore on. At home later, after I made some comments I'm not proud of, I learned that lunch at 11:15 was exactly right, but he was waiting for me to come by the office to walk to the restaurant with him. Ooops."

Conflict #_____

SCENARIO #4

"She helped put me through dental school, and since the first day, she's always been a big help in my practice. But now that our youngest is going off to college, she wants to go to graduate school, get her Ph.D., and teach at the university. Who would cover when my receptionist has a sick toddler and can't come in? Who would oversee my billing? And would our home life be the same? She doesn't understand why I'm not keen on her idea."

Conflict #_____

SCENARIO #5

"His favorite verse, he'd always joked, was 'Wives, be submissive to your husbands' but living with him was no joke! It wasn't too long after the honeymoon that I started feeling more like a doormat than a bride. He didn't seem to care about my opinion on anything, and any efforts I made at home were never good enough. When his nicknames for me became less than affectionate, I thought we needed counseling."

Conflict #_____

SCENARIO #6

"He teaches all day long, and twice a week he teaches in the evening at the community college. I know his day is crammed full of people, but I stay home with a six-month-old. Oh, sure, my part-time accounting gives me something to do during naptime, but it doesn't get me in touch with people. So when Todd comes home, I'm ready to talk—and talk and talk, he'd say—and I always have ideas about fun things to do with friends and family on weekends. It's like pulling teeth to get him to even want to do something."

Conflict #_____

"Humility and grace are the two most important attitudes that the Bible suggests in dealing with someone else's sin. Go tough on the issue but soft on the person."

- What is humility?
- What is grace?
- Why would these be key to dealing with your spouse's sin—or, for that matter, with any other kind of conflict?

TIME FOR THOUGHT

Getting to the Real Issue

DIRECTIONS

Read through the questions on the next few pages, taking this opportunity to analyze a recent or current conflict in your marriage and what you can do to resolve it.

You'll have 8 minutes to read and think about this section, which will be a helpful tool in the future as other conflicts arise. And it can help you today! Choose a specific conflict in your marriage and begin developing a plan of action for resolving it.

1. Describe a current conflict in your marriage.

   Sparks fly whenever we discuss...

   _____

   _____

   _____

   _____

   _____

2. Which of the following categories does the above conflict fit?

   - Conflict #1: The Sin of One Spouse
   - Conflict #2: The Immaturity or Brokenness of One Person
   - Conflict #3: Hurt Feelings That Are No One's Fault
   - Conflict #4: Conflicting Desires
   - Conflict #5: Desires of One Person Versus the Needs of the Relationship
   - Conflict #6: Known Versus Unknown Problems

   Now that I think about it, I think the real issue was/is. . . .

   Conflict #_____

3. Looking below, find the path toward resolution for the conflict you just identified. What are you responsible for doing in order to resolve the conflict? Be specific about your plan of action.

Conflict #1: Sin of One Spouse

Humility and grace are the two most important attitudes that the Bible suggests in dealing with someone else's sin. Go tough on the issue, but—as God does with you—go soft on the person as you work through this process:

1. Rid yourself of judgmentalism, condemnation, shame, or pride.

2. Speak to the issue directly. Let your spouse know that you know about the sin and tell him that what he is doing is not right.

3. Accept an apology if it is forthcoming, and offer forgiveness.

4. When emotions are not strong, talk about the problem to see if further help is needed.

5. Agree on a follow-up plan: "If I notice something again, what do you want me to do?"

    Plan of action:

    My first step this week:

Conflict #2:
Immaturity or Brokenness of One Person

In every relationship, the reality of the two people involved eventually surfaces. When it does, it is very important to face that reality—the immaturity and brokenness—in the following helpful ways.

1. Accept reality about yourself and your spouse. Both of you will be unprepared for some of the realities life brings.

2. Communicate your support to your spouse. We do not grow when we are judged, nagged, condemned, resented, or subjected to some other lack of grace. We all need to feel that someone is on our side and supporting us (1 Thessalonians 5:14).

3. Face issues as real problems. Part of love is honesty and requiring holiness and growth from each other. So where your spouse is not mature, let her know.

4. Own your problems. If you are the one confronted with your immaturity, own it. Be a "boundary lover."

5. Get help. We all need help, mentoring, support, and teaching. No one ever grew up on his own.

6. Make it mutual. Guard against labeling one spouse "the problem person." This is never true. Neither one of you is a complete person yet; you are both still growing up.

Plan of action:

My first step this week:

Conflict #3:
Hurt Feelings That Are No One's Fault

Here are some hints in how to deal with hurt when no one is really "wrong."

1. When you are hurt, acknowledge it to yourself. Know yourself well enough to know when something is bothering you, and own your feelings.

2. Communicate. Tell your spouse that you are hurt by something she did. But don't blame your spouse as if she has sinned.

3. Empathize. If you are on the other end of the hurt, show empathy for your spouse's feelings. Know that by caring and offering empathy you are not saying that it is your "fault."

4. Identify patterns and plan. If you learn what hurts you, then you can anticipate things that might hurt you in the future. When it happens, you can take precautions to respond helpfully or, better yet, avoid the hurt altogether.

5. Be in a healing mode. We are all responsible for the hurts we carry around inside.

6. Guard against "going to court." Don't waste time and energy trying to find out who was "wrong." Right and wrong is not an issue here. Instead, become a healing agent, with empathy, understanding, nondefensiveness, and care.

    Plan of action:

    My first step this week:

Conflict #4: Conflicting Desires

Normally, two people develop a pattern of give and take, and differences get negotiated. But sometimes they hit a stalemate. A few principles can help.

1. Avoid moralizing your preference. Humans tend to see what they prefer as right, especially if one of the preferences has a moral-sounding quality to it. Make sure you realize that your desire is not a higher one than your spouse's.

2. Empathize with and understand the importance of your spouse's desires. Avoid devaluing what your spouse wants. Validate her desires as real and good.

3. Seek to make sure that your spouse gets his or her desires met before yours are met, and you will avoid most arguments. (In reality, this is not going to happen often, but your attitude is what is important.)

4. If necessary, keep an account of yours, mine, and ours. If you keep an account, you will guard against the passive spouse becoming the perpetual loser. The more assertive one will finally get some limits.

5. Don't define an "I" choice as a "we" choice. Make sure that when you want your spouse to do a "we" thing, he or she is really wanting to do that as well. If not, and he or she goes along, remember it is for you and not for the both of you. Count it in your own column.

6. Make sure "we's" are agreed upon. Both of you should sign off on activities that are really for the two of you. When you both have to sacrifice for something, make sure that you are on the same page in wanting it and agreeing to it.

7. Question your preferences. Some of the things on which you take strong stances may not be true desires. As James tells us, we sometimes want things for wrong motives (James 4:3).

8. Expand and grow. Instead of fighting for your own way, give in to the preference of your spouse as a learning and stretching experience. Try to see the activity through your spouse's eyes and you might learn to enjoy something you never thought possible.

    Plan of action:

    My first step this week:

Conflict #5:
Desires of One Person Versus the Needs of the Relationship

Sometimes the desire of one spouse conflicts with the needs of the relationship. Problems arise when the marriage always serves one member and never the other. In the end, the marriage benefits as each member grows, but keep it in balance, making sure that the marriage gets served first. Here are some hints.

1. Remember that the marriage comes first. Give the best to the relationship before your individual desires.

2. Be clear about what you want. Tell your spouse clearly.

3. Be excited about what your spouse wants for himself or herself individually.

4. Make sure that your individual desires that take away from the relationship over the long haul are not unbalanced in terms of what your spouse gets.

5. As much as possible, make long-term plans for individual things that take away from the marriage. This way you can plan together to sacrifice.

Plan of action:

My first step this week:

Conflict #6:
Known Versus Unknown Problems

We all have aspects of our personalities and character that we do not know about. The trick to growth is becoming partner to this secret knowledge. There is a difference between known and unknown problems, however, and they should be handled differently.

1. Conflict in Known Problems
   - If you have talked about a certain pattern before, agree about what you will do if the pattern returns. In principle, the person knows that he has the problem and should be working on it.
   - If you have talked before and want each other's help, then confronting will be used not for policing but for making someone aware: "I cannot see when I am doing that. Please let me know."
   - If you know about the problem, the plan to fix it is your responsibility. Don't blame your spouse in any way for something that you already know about yourself.
   - If it is your partner's problem and she knows it, don't enable her. Follow through with the consequences you have agreed upon.

2. Conflict in Unknown Problems
   - Agree with each other that you have permission to tell each other about what you notice.

- When you are confronted, be open. Don't be defensive. Accept the feedback, at least agreeing to look at yourself and see if it is true.
- Seek feedback from others also.
- Ask your spouse to show you each time it happens so that you can see the pattern.
- Give grace to each other. Change is not going to be immediate. Give your spouse time.

Plan of action:

My first step this week:

VIDEO SEGMENT
Resolving Conflict

- "Boundary resisters" are people who are not open to feedback, who cannot see when they are wrong, who do not like limits of any kind, and who blame everyone else for their problems.

- "Boundary lovers" are people who have the ability to hear feedback and listen. If you have an attitude of openness and a desire for your spouse and you to experience freedom and love, then you will be able to talk through problems and help each other.

- Conflict is normal.

- The Bible suggests the following predictable path for resolving all kinds of conflicts:

  1. Observation. You can't fix a problem you do not see. One of you has to notice the problem first and see it as a problem or conflict.
  2. Confrontation. You can't fix a problem you don't talk about. Speak honestly with each other, but speak the truth in love as you let your spouse know what is wrong.
  3. Ownership, grief, and apology. If you are the problem—or at least part of it—own it. If you have been hurt, own your hurt and communicate it. If you are the one who is doing the hurting, then confess and apologize. If you are the wounded party, forgive as well as express your hurt.
  4. Repentance. Once you see your part in something, repent. In short, stop it. Commit to change.
  5. Involvement in the process. Problems do not go away immediately, so become involved in whatever

process will be necessary for change. It may be counseling or some other form of structured help, but commit to it and stay involved.

6. Reexamination. Have some system of reexamination. Just because you have faced something doesn't mean it is gone forever. Get a checkup from those to whom you have made yourself accountable. And then continue to get reexamined for other things as well.

- Conflict can still be painful even if everyone is open to feedback. So remember and follow the basic rules of communication:

  1. Listen and seek to understand the other before you seek to be understood.
  2. Actively empathize and use reflective listening to let the other person know you understand.
  3. Do not devalue or explain away what the other person is feeling or saying. Don't defend; just listen.
  4. Clarify to make sure you understand. Ask questions.
  5. Use "I" statements that show you are taking responsibility for what you are feeling or wanting.

- Don't be afraid of conflict. There is always a death before a resurrection and conflict before deeper intimacy. Go through it lovingly, and chances are you will find more intimacy with your mate on the other side.

TIME TO TALK

It's All in the Delivery

DIRECTIONS

Split into groups of four or five. You will have 8 minutes to work through the questions below with your group, allowing everyone in the group to contribute.

1. Dr. Cloud's closing admonition was "Don't be afraid of conflict." Why are some of us afraid of conflict?

2. Review the basic rules for communication that Dr. Cloud outlined for us on page 114. What are some of the benefits of communicating according to these guidelines? What problems are avoided?

3. What guideline calls for new behavior or a new attitude on your part?

TIME FOR THOUGHT
Working Through It

1. Who are you—a boundary lover or a boundary resister?
   - Are you usually not open to feedback?
   - Do you have trouble seeing when you are wrong?
   - Do you tend to not like limits of any kind?
   - Do you blame everyone else for your problems?

   If you identified with most of the points above, you're a boundary resister. Give a few details from your life as evidence.

   - Do you have the ability to hear feedback and listen?
   - Are you open to what people have to say to you and about you?
   - Do you take responsibility for your problems and mistakes?
   - Do you want your spouse and you to experience freedom and love?

   If you identified with most of these points, then you are a boundary lover. Give a few details from your life as evidence.

2. Is your spouse a boundary lover or a boundary resister? What supporting evidence do you see in your mate's behavior? Be specific.

3. The Bible suggests the following path for resolving all kinds of conflicts. As you read through the steps and answer the questions, see where the Lord seems to be taking you and, in faith, act on what you need to do.

A. Observation. You can't fix a problem you do not see.

- Are you aware of a problem that your spouse does not yet see? Why have you been quiet about it?

- Could your spouse be aware of a problem you don't yet see? How would you like to respond if and when your mate brings it up? What will you do to invite that discussion?

B. Confrontation. You can't fix a problem you don't talk about.

- When have you been slow to talk with your spouse about a problem? How did your hesitation impact the problem and your relationship with your spouse?

- Using either a hypothetical problem or one you currently face in your marriage, practice speaking the truth to your spouse and doing so in love. What will you say and how will you say it?

C. Ownership, grief, and apology. If you are the problem—or at least part of it—own it. If you have been hurt, own your hurt and communicate it. If you are the one who is doing the hurting, then confess and apologize. If you are the wounded party, forgive as well as express your hurt.

- Into which category—the problem, the wounded spouse, or the wounding one—do you currently fall? According to this list, what should you do—and when will you do it?

- When have you not acted according to this formula of ownership, grief, apology, and forgiveness? What impact did your actions have on your marriage relationship?

D. Repentance. Once you see your part in something, repent.
   - When has your "repentance" been merely a matter of words? What impact did this pseudo-repentance have on your relationship with your spouse?

   - Genuine repentance requires action: a change in direction, a change in behavior. What repentance, if any, is it your responsibility to be living out now? Be specific about the actions you will take to do so.

E. Involvement in the process. Problems do not go away immediately. Become involved in whatever process will be necessary for change.
   - Think back on a problem you and your spouse have encountered. Describe the process of change involved in resolving the problem. What did that process demand of you? Be specific. What might have happened in your

marriage had you not gotten or stayed involved in resolving the problem?

- What current problem in your marriage will challenge you to get and stay involved in the process of resolving it? What will you do to be sure you persevere?

F. Reexamination. Have some system of reexamination. Get a checkup from those to whom you have made yourself accountable. And then continue to get reexamined for other things as well.

   - Consider past problems in your marriage. Give an example of one that recurred to some degree. What might have prevented that recurrence?

   - Who can reexamine you for any recurrence of a past issue? When will you talk to that person/those people? What benefits do you think will come from such reexamination?

- Prayer is key to solving any conflict. Here is a sample to help guide your conversation with the Lord.

   Holy and heavenly Father, help me to see problems that are my responsibility to address and then to speak about them in truth and love. Enable me to own the problems which are my responsibility to own, to own any hurt I may feel, to confess and apologize when I'm hurting my mate, and to forgive my mate when I'm the one being hurt. Strengthen my resolve to truly repent, to change my actions and not merely say the words. Grant me the ability to persevere. Fill me with the grace I need for times of reexamination as well as for those times when my mate and I are working on our marriage. Also, Lord, may your Spirit work in me so that I can seek to understand my mate before seeking to be understood; actively empathize with my spouse; and listen instead of rushing to defend myself. Make me more like Christ. Amen.

Closing Prayer

Lord God, thank you that you are ever-present in this challenging relationship of marriage where conflict is indeed inevitable. I pray, Lord, for the grace to live by the Golden Rule and the courage to die to self and to self-centeredness as I deal with conflict. I ask you, too, to grant me the sense of humor and perspective necessary to keep me from majoring on the minors. And prompt me, Lord, to call on you for wisdom and patience, kindness and love as I seek to have you grow me and mature me through conflict. I pray in Jesus' name. Amen.

Boundary Building

1. What, if anything, can you affirm about the way your spouse handles conflict? Offer affirmation if you can.

2. In the exercise It's All in the Delivery on page 115, you reviewed basic rules for communication. What skill for better communication are you going to sharpen this week? What will you do towards that end?

3. Spend some more time this week on the "Working Through It" suggestions for resolving conflict, whether your spouse is a boundary lover or a boundary resister.

Some Warning Signs to Help Your Marriage

OVERVIEW

In this session, you will

- Be called to actively protect your marriage because conflict and hurt, the emotional intimacy of marriage, not knowing your limits, taking the marriage for granted, problems in setting boundaries with one another, and the inability to live with differences can allow intruders into a marriage.

- Realize that work, friends, kids, church, outside hobbies and interests, parents/in-laws, television, the Internet, financial involvement, sports, shopping, addictions, and, worst of all, affairs are common intruders.

- Be reminded that boundaries were not designed to end relationships, but to preserve and deepen them.

- Look at the connection between boundaries and suffering; boundaries and problem solving in a marriage; boundaries and the issue of submission; and boundaries and divorce.

VIDEO SEGMENT

No Trespassing!

- The marriage union itself needs to be actively protected. That's where boundaries come in. We need, for instance, to have boundaries between our marriage and the outside world. It is our responsibility to say no to third parties—to making a best friend or secretary the confidant, to investing more in one's parents or children than one's spouse.

- A life of "yes" to everything else ultimately results in a "no" to your marriage. Marriage means doing some hard work in forsaking, or leaving behind, other things.

- Marriage was not designed to be the source of all life for us. All good marriages need outside support, so seek out the right and appropriate sources. Your sources of love should not only be helping you but also be helping you love your mate.

- Often the intruder isn't the issue. The intruder is the result, or symptom, of another issue in marriage. The real issue has more to do with your relationship or your character.

- When a marriage contains conflict or hurt, we tend to busy ourselves in other people and activities. When you become aware of this situation in your marriage, it is your responsibility to bring the real issue to light and deal with it.

- The nature of emotional intimacy itself can make a marriage vulnerable to outside influences. When we notice our vulnerability and exposure, we become frightened. Or, when intimacy does its work, one spouse may pull away from what the other spouse reveals about hurts, failings, or sins.

- Some other things that allow intruders into a marriage include the following:

  — Not knowing your limits. Often couples have problems with intruders because one or both of the mates simply are not aware of their own time, energy, and investment resources and don't have enough left for their marriage.

  — Taking the marriage for granted. Some people are unaware of the fragility of marriage. They often adopt the mentality that no crises are going on, so everything's okay. This is an immature perspective.

  — Problems in setting boundaries with one another. If your spouse is irresponsible or hurtful, it is your responsibility to maintain a position of love without rescue and of truth without nagging.

  — An inability to live with differences. Being different should be a benefit in a marriage. The danger comes when a spouse goes outside the marriage because of these differences.

- Work, friends, kids, church, outside hobbies and interests, parents, in-laws, television, the Internet, financial involvement, sports, shopping, addictions, and, the worst of all, affairs are some common intruders in a marriage.

- If and when these intruders appear in your marriage, evaluate how they fit into the marriage, how they affect the less-involved spouse, and then negotiate a compromise so that both people can love and grow.

TIME TO TALK

A Plan of Protection

DIRECTIONS

Split into groups of three or four and discuss the questions below. You will have 5 minutes for this exercise.

1. What does it mean that "A marriage is only as strong as what it costs to protect it"?

2. Some intruders that can weaken the marriage bond are work, friends, kids, church, outside hobbies and interests, parents/in-laws, television, the Internet, financial involvement, sports, shopping, addictions, and, the worst of all, affairs.

   • What makes a marriage strong against intruders?

   • What in the past has made it difficult for you to strengthen your marriage's boundaries? Lack of awareness or information? Busyness? Fear of closeness? Something else?

TIME FOR THOUGHT

Saying Yes to Your Marriage

DIRECTIONS

On your own, review and answer the questions below. You will have 10 minutes to work on this section.

1. Most of us would like to avoid having to say no in life. It's work, it causes anxiety, and it can upset people. Yet reality dictates that in order to say yes to keeping a close marriage, you will have to say no to lots of other things. A life of "yes" to everything else ultimately results in a "no" to your marriage.

    *   What recent decision was a "yes" to something else and a "no" to your marriage?

    *   Why did you make that decision?

2. All "intruder" problems are ultimately caused by either adding the wrong thing (inappropriate people or bad influences) to the marriage, subtracting the good (closeness and honesty) from the marriage, or both. What is your diagnosis of any "intruder" problems you're facing now or have faced before?

3. When a marriage contains conflict or hurt, we tend to busy ourselves in other people and activities. Activity can anesthetize the deficits and pain in the marital connection.

- Think for a moment about how busy you are. What indications, if any, do you have that it is an unhealthy busyness for you and/or your marriage? A close friend might help you evaluate your busyness.

- When, if ever, have date nights and getaways (important to nourish a marriage) been disappointing because of unresolved conflicts?

- What did you do—or, if the situation is current, what could you do—to bring the real issue to light and deal with it?

4. Some intruders that can weaken the marriage bond are work, friends, kids, church, outside hobbies and interests, parents/in-laws, television, the Internet, financial involvement, sports, shopping, addictions, and, the worst of all, affairs.

   - Which of these intruders threaten your marriage bond?

   - What do you do, or could you do, to continually invest in your attachment to your spouse? To keep your love secure and safe?

VIDEO SEGMENT
The Misuse of Boundaries

- Like any good thing, boundaries can be misused. Boundaries were not designed to end relationships, but to preserve and deepen them.

- Sometimes when we set limits in marriage, we suffer more, not less. But such suffering is designed to help us adapt to reality.

- Ungodly suffering comes from either doing the wrong thing or not doing the right thing. But godly suffering causes us to grow.

- God wants you to end the ungodly suffering in your life, which produces no growth, and enter his suffering, which always brings good results. So set limits to build love, honesty, and freedom in your marriage.

- Boundaries can help you solve problems in your marriage. Consider these steps:

  — Love: When problems arise in your marriage, the first thing to do is to establish that you desire the best for your mate, even if he has not been a loving person himself.

  — Others: Not only is it your responsibility to speak from love, but it is your responsibility to be receiving care, support, and encouragement from God and others outside your marriage.

  — Ownership: There are almost no marriage problems in which one spouse contributes one hundred percent and the other, zero percent. So ask yourself what you have contributed or are contributing to the problem.

— Invitation: Whatever the problem between you and your spouse, invite him to change. With empathy and love, request that he make a specific change.

— Warning: When you warn your spouse, you tell him that something painful might happen in the future and that his behavior will help determine what happens.

— Patience: Silent suffering is not patience. Patience allows the process to happen while you are providing love and truth, the ingredients of growth.

— Consequence: When love, support, invitation, warning, and patience are in place, you may have to follow through on your consequence. Consequences protect you and also help your spouse deal with the reality of his actions.

— Renegotiation: Many boundaries can be changed over time as a spouse matures and changes.

— Forgiveness: Finally, be actively and constantly in the process of forgiveness. It is your responsibility to both forgive your spouse and request forgiveness from your spouse.

• Marriages that work best have equal, interdependent partners with differing roles.

• Few passages in the Bible have been subject to more misunderstanding and misuse than Ephesians 5:22–23, 25. In the Bible, however, leadership does not mean domination. The idea of submission is never meant to allow someone to overstep another's boundaries.

- A leader is a giving servant who is committed to the best of those he or she is leading. If a wife is resisting a husband who is loving, truthful, protective, and providing for her well-being, then something is wrong. If you and your spouse are not using your freedom and boundaries to serve each other, then you do not understand love. Love is not self-seeking. Freely seek each other's best, and submission issues will disappear.

- Divorce is not a boundary in a relationship; divorce is an end to a relationship. God's solution for "I can't live that way anymore" is basically "Good! Don't live that way anymore. Do marriage my way." God's way means acting on the behaviors suggested in the following three questions:

  — What can you do to set firm limits against evil behavior?

  — What can you do to get the love and support you need from other places?

  — What can you do to suffer long but in the right way?

- Boundaries in marriage seek to change and redeem the relationship. Divorce should never be the first boundary. It is your responsibility to set boundaries in the context of relationship, not for the purpose of ending relationship. Use boundaries to end your suffering and then use those boundaries to bring about redemption and reconciliation as well.

TIME TO INTERACT
Lessons from Life

SUBMISSION

As the video suggested, leadership does not mean domination. Marriages that work best have equal, interdependent partners with differing roles. The idea of submission is never meant to allow someone to overstep another's boundaries. A leader is a giving servant who is committed to the best of the one(s) he or she is leading. If a wife is resisting a husband who is loving, truthful, protective, and providing for her well-being, then something is wrong. Likewise, if a husband isn't loving, truthful, protective, and providing for his wife's well-being, something is wrong.

1. What new understanding or greater appreciation of submission do you have as a result of this teaching?

2. Read Ephesians 5:22–23, 25. Focus on yourself, the only person you can change, and not on your spouse: What changes in yourself—in your attitudes, actions, words—could you make in light of this passage from Ephesians?

SUFFERING

Suffering, at least the kind God has called us to experience, is designed to help us adapt to reality the way it really is.

1. What lessons have you learned in the school of suffering? What reality has suffering helped you adapt to? Be specific about the lesson and how you learned it.

2. What lessons have you learned from any pain you've known in your marriage? Again be specific about the lesson and how you learned it.

What lesson could you be learning from some present struggle or pain in your marriage?

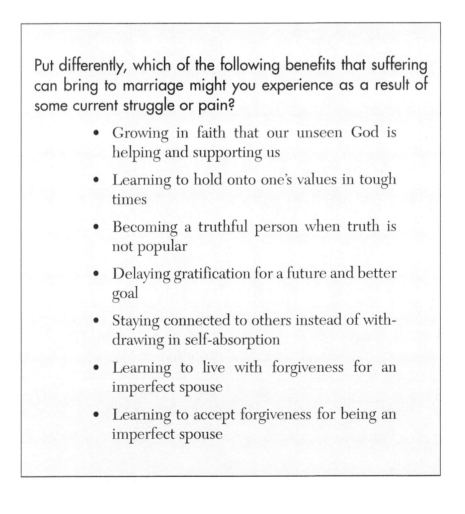

Put differently, which of the following benefits that suffering can bring to marriage might you experience as a result of some current struggle or pain?

- Growing in faith that our unseen God is helping and supporting us

- Learning to hold onto one's values in tough times

- Becoming a truthful person when truth is not popular

- Delaying gratification for a future and better goal

- Staying connected to others instead of withdrawing in self-absorption

- Learning to live with forgiveness for an imperfect spouse

- Learning to accept forgiveness for being an imperfect spouse

TIME FOR ACTION

Boundaries as Tools for Problem-Solving

DIRECTIONS

Boundaries can help us both guard against ungodly suffering and benefit from the godly suffering that teaches us lessons and helps us adapt to reality. Boundaries can also help couples solve problems they encounter in their marriage. On your own, think through and answer the questions below. You will have 15 minutes for this exercise.

Love. When problems arise in marriage, the first thing to do is to establish that you desire the best for your mate, even if he has not been a loving person himself.

1. Does your mate clearly understand that you desire the best for him? If so, what did you do to establish that fact in his mind?

2. If not, what will you do to make it clear that you are working on boundaries because you desire the best for him?

Others. Not only is it your responsibility to speak from love, but it is also your responsibility to be receiving care, support, and encouragement from God and others outside your marriage.

1. With whom outside your marriage are you connected? From whom are you receiving the care, support, and encouragement you need as you do this important boundary work in your marriage? Or where will you go to find such supportive relationships?

2. What are you doing to stay connected to God as you work on boundaries in your marriage? What might strengthen that connection?

Ownership. There are almost no marriage problems in which one spouse contributes one hundred percent and the other, zero percent.

1. Step back from your marriage or ask a close friend for a more objective perspective. What have you contributed or are you contributing to the boundary issues in your marriage?

2. What can you do to own the problem, take responsibility for it, and improve the situation? Also, how does this ownership change your attitude toward your spouse?

Invitation.

1. Whatever the problem between you and your spouse, invite him to change before you set limits. With empathy and love, request that he make a change. Invitation can preclude having to set some consequence.

2. What would be an appropriate invitation for you to extend to your spouse right now?

3. Exactly what will you say—and how will you say it? Your delivery is key!

Warning. When we warn our spouse, we tell him that something painful might happen in the future and that his behavior will help determine what happens.

1. Assuming your spouse does not accept your invitation to change, what warning will you give him or her?

2. What "something painful . . . in the future" would be a logical or natural consequence for your spouse's unchanging behavior?

Patience. Silent suffering is not patience. Patience allows the process to happen while you are providing love and truth, the ingredients of growth.

1. In what efforts to change have you personally experienced God's patience?

2. In response to God's patience with you (2 Peter 3:9), what will you do to show your spouse patience, to be loving and truthful, while you allow him time to grow? Be specific about what you will stop and what you will start doing and saying.

Consequence. When love, support, invitation, warning, and patience are in place, you may have to follow through on your consequence. Consequences protect you and also help your spouse deal with the reality of his actions.

1. Boundaries should not grow out of anger, revenge, or punishment. Have yours? A close friend may offer you a reality check.

2. What consequences would be helpful to put into place right now?

3. In what relationship(s) will you find the strength you need to be consistent as you enforce boundaries with your spouse?

Renegotiation. Many boundaries can be changed over time as a spouse matures and changes. What you make external can become internalized in your marriage, as it becomes a part of who you two are.

1. What boundaries, if any, have you renegotiated through the years as you or your spouse has grown?

2. The more people grow, the fewer rules they need. When have you seen this to be true in real life, perhaps in your own life or in the life of children?

3. "In marriage, try to operate with as few rules as possible." Why is this good advice?

4. What current boundaries would you be wise to renegotiate? Be specific about the changes—and about when you will make them.

Forgiveness. Finally, be actively and constantly in the process of forgiveness. To forgive is to cancel a debt. It is your responsibility to both forgive your spouse and request forgiveness from your spouse.

1. Setting boundaries involves risks that can disrupt the process of marriage growth. Which disruptions listed below do you tend to bump up against in your marriage? Why?
   • Blaming
   • Judging
   • Laying guilt trips on your spouse
   • Being unable to let go of past problems
   • Taking too much responsibility for your spouse's issues

2. What will you do to more consciously, more genuinely live in forgiveness? What, for instance, might become a regular prayer?

Closing Prayer

Father God and Redeemer God, first I ask you to show me where I've misunderstood your purposes in suffering, misconstrued your definition of submission, and misused boundaries in my marriage. Show me where I'm doing wrong or not doing right. Forgive me for letting things interfere with my commitment to my spouse and drain me of time and energy that I should invest in my marriage. Help me to make a daily investment in my marriage. And, in order to keep our love safe and secure, help me to set and maintain boundaries between my marriage and the outside world. Protect us from intruders. Help me—help us—to say no to the things that intrude, things like busyness, work, friends, and kids—so that our marriage may be more what you intend it to be. In Jesus' name. Amen.

Boundary Building

1. Review this concluding session, finish the "Boundaries as Tools for Problem-Solving" if you haven't already, and then look back through the other seven sessions.

2. Which points from this week's session are you going to act on? Be specific about what you will do.

3. Which points from the eight-week course do you especially want to remember and live out in your marriage? What will you do? Again, be specific. You might even ask someone to hold you accountable by asking how you're doing in a month, three months, and six months.

4. Which prayers in this guide do you want to keep praying regularly? Don't feel you have to use the prayers in
   their entirety. Pull out those lines which are especially
   meaningful.

Embark on a
Life-Changing Journey
of Personal and Spiritual Growth

DR. HENRY CLOUD   **DR. JOHN TOWNSEND**

Dr. Henry Cloud and Dr. John Townsend have been bringing hope and healing to millions for over two decades. They have helped people everywhere discover solutions to life's most difficult personal and relational challenges. Their material provides solid, practical answers and offers guidance in the areas of *parenting, singles issues, personal growth,* and *leadership.*

Bring either Dr. Cloud or Dr. Townsend to your church or organization. They are available for:

- Seminars on a wide variety of topics
- Training for small group leaders
- Conferences
- Educational events
- Consulting with your organization

Other opportunities to experience Dr. Cloud and Dr. Townsend:

- Ultimate Leadership workshops—held in Southern California throughout the year
- Small group curriculum
- Seminars via Satellite
- Solutions Audio Club—Solutions is a weekly recorded presentation

For other resources, and for dates of seminars and workshops
by Dr. Cloud and Dr. Townsend, visit:
www.cloudtownsend.com

For other information **Call (800) 676-HOPE (4673)**

Or write to:
Cloud-Townsend Resources
18092 Sky Park South, Suite A
Irvine, CA 92614

About the Writer

Lisa Guest has been writing, editing, and developing curriculum since 1984. She holds a master's degree in English literature from UCLA and teaches at her church whenever the opportunity arises. She lives in Irvine, California, with her husband and three children.